I0422157

The Ordinary Guide to Writing Your Extraordinary Book

By S. J. Russell

DEDICATION

It's for you and others like you that yearn
to say something in the form of written
words that caused this book to exist.

ACKNOWLEGEMENTS

This book was written comprised of
personal condensed notes from classes
using the following books as teaching
materials;
Characters and Viewpoint by Orson Scott
Card
Beginnings, Middles & Ends by Nancy
Kress
Plot by Ansen Dibell
Scene and Structure by Jack M. Bickham
As well as internet searches using Google
and Wikipedia.

And as always and forever-Thanks,
Wonderful.

INTRODUCTION

Honesty is good. It's sometimes harsh, but using it is always for the best. Having this belief, I want to state clearly, I'm not an authority on writing fiction books. I'm a beginner, newbie, holdin on for dear life, struggling and easily confused novice. I'm just an ordinary hopefully helpful person that really likes books.

Years ago, probably just like you are now, I wanted to know how to write a book. So, I got a diploma on how to write books-in creative writing. While taking classes, I made a crazy amount of notes. Not being a genius, I wanted to simplify what I was learning so I could retain it. Through my work, all the incredibly thick reference materials became condensed to clear paragraphs, sometimes thinned down to one thought provoking question.

After my classes, I read and read lots of other literature on how to write books to attempt to perfect my art. Nonfiction books that possibly thought I was an Idiot or a Dummy. I had purchased them because I thought perhaps, I was those things. Because without referencing my notes, I got off track easily. Perhaps you do too. I used my notes as a guide as I wrote my first book and self-published.

A couple of years later, I attended the first meeting of my area's writers group. Having met a dozen other want to be authors in a tiny town where I thought I was probably the only one, I had a thought. If my small town had a dozen, then the number statistically in the neighboring larger city, the amount in our county, state, country, the world must be astronomical. It seems logically, there are a lot of people out there that want to write a book. They want to tell a thrilling story to others, teach lessons or just share. I think that's extraordinary and beautiful.

And I want to help. But as I said before I'm no one of consequence. All I've got are these notes that have really helped me. These ordinary notes, I thought to myself, might help somebody else- so... I wrote "The Ordinary Guide To Writing Your Extraordinary Book". I sincerely hope that it helps you accomplish all that you attempt in the literary world. I look forward to reading it. Because again, I really like books.

The great 88, once I organized and cleaned up my scribbles and notes, it broke down to about 88 simple questions to ask yourself or relatively easy steps to accomplish as you move forward in your fiction book writing project. I have put only a few steps per page leaving plenty of room to make your own notes. Here's the ordinary guide to writing your extraordinary book...

STEP ONE:
Create a main character- Your Antagonist/hero.
This is usually the character or one of the characters that comes to mind first.

STEP TWO:
Create the main character's opposition- Your Protagonist/villain.
Almost everything needs balance. The yin to the yang, the other matching bookend. Please don't underestimate the value and necessity of the villain. He/she/it must be just as interesting as your hero. He/she/it must evoke as much hate as your hero does love.

STEP THREE:
Decide how many characters are needed for your particular story.

STEP FOUR:
Create all major characters.
Create Main characters that give the Reader a reason to care about them, make them believable/easy to understand

so the Reader can become emotionally involved with them.

STEP FIVE:
Create all minor characters.

STEP SIX:
Have at least one very strong female character. Possibly a positive representation of a minority if it fits your vision for your tale. Not only is this good for society-publishers look for it.
Some writers use stereotypes by working with them, while other writers surprise the Reader by playing against them. You decide.

STEP SEVEN:
Give your characters names. Please try to avoid having names that start with the same letter such as Ted/Tina or names with the same length or sound such as Kim/Jim. This confuses Readers easily.

STEP EIGHT:
Give Major characters a convincing motive and a past.

Motive is what the character does or has intentions of doing.

The Past is what the character has done or what has been done to them.

STEP NINE:
Give all characters work/careers (what he/she/it does as a job and why)

STEP TEN:
Give all characters relationships and a network of friends/coworkers/neighbors.
Give your characters the six degrees of Kevin Bacon treatment. - loosely connect them to each other.

STEP ELEVEN:
Give major characters interesting weakness and flaws.

Example: Physical handicaps or like me in my twenties- a mild addiction to Dr. Pepper.

STEP TWELVE:
Give major characters special talents and tastes.
A big part of who your characters are, is what they can do.

STEP THIRTEEN:
Give major characters compelling habits and/or reputations.
Reputation whether deserved or not, is part of a character's identity.

STEP FOURTEEN:
Give major characters an interior space or landscape.
Ask yourself-where do my characters live/sleep?

STEP FIFTEEN:
Choose which characters will have sexual

tensions, if any.

STEP SIXTEEN:
Give major characters an object to be associated with, to carry or use often. This makes them more memorable.

STEP SEVENTEEN:
Give major characters different personalities around others (how they act at work/on the phone/in public versus at home/with their lover/around children and pets, etc.) This makes them more realistic.

STEP EIGHTEEN:
Choose a part of each major character's life to become unbearable as the story escalates.

STEP NINETEEN:
Write a self-concept for each Major character in 15 words or less.
This helps you home in on who everyone really is in your story.

STEP TWENTY PART 1:
If necessary, choose other details about all characters such as social class, religion, education level and physical description such as age, height, weight, eye and hair color), if they own a pet and what kind, place in family (only child, the baby, etc.)

Please Note: When writing, try not to focus too much on physical descriptions, because, readers will love a hero no matter what they look like. The color of his/her hair or eyes is not that relevant to most stories.

In fact, there are many fantastic books out there that never describe their main character's physical attributes at all and let the reader imagine how the characters look themselves. You decide if this is important and how much.

STEP TWENTY PART 2:
Write all character info including the self-concept done on step 19 onto a worksheet/character card for you to reference as you write.

STEP TWENTY-ONE:
Decide what factors to focus on in each of your chapters as you write. This is not your overall theme but the factors you want to see more often than others in your chapters/certain places in your story.

Keeping it simple, basically there are four factors, some refer to them as components or elements.
What you need to decide is what you want your reader to pay attention to in certain parts of your story. This is what professors like to call M.I.C.E.- which is an acronym, an icky initial thing to help students remember the factors of Milieu, Idea, Character and Event.

Milieu Factor.
Milieu is defined as a character's social environment. It's the world, planet, society, weather, family, laws, cultures, customs- all the elements of a special place and its people. If you want the Reader to notice this most often in your story, you want to write focused on the factor of Milieu in several chapters.

Idea Factor.
Idea stories are about the process of finding information. A problem or question is asked in the beginning of the story and usually revealed at the end. If you want your reader to think or become engrossed in a mystery or discovery often you want to write focused on the factor of idea in several chapters.

Character Factor.
Character stories are about the transformation of a character and his or her role. It's the nature of what they do and why they do it. In these stories, the character's life becomes unbearable and the story's focus is on how he/she/it deals with that. If you want your readers to see a character overcoming obstacles often, write with a focus on the factor of Character in several chapters.

Event Factor.
Event stories focus on, you guessed it, an event. Usually an event which disrupts the natural order and causes a state of flux. It's a story about trying to restore the old

order of things or building a new one. If you want your Reader focused on a natural disaster, a dramatic family ripping divorce or any other traumatic event and their effects, then your focus should be on the factor of Event in several chapters.

Please note. You can write with all four factors focused upon throughout all your chapters. A good example of this is Lord of the Rings. But having to choose one to focus on through several chapters helps you determine what is really important to the story you want to tell.

STEP TWENTY-TWO PART 1:
Decide if your book should be Representational or Presentational.

Representational.
The story is represented by a main character. This enhances the illusion that the story being read is true. It's much easier for the reader to become emotionally involved. Everything is seen from a character's point of view. But there's no narrator to supply info that the character doesn't know.

Presentational:
The story is presented by a narrator. It's close to impossible to forget that the story is fictional but easier to present clear ideas. All the characters are talked about by a narrator. This is best suited for comedy because it has less emotional involvement.

STEP TWENTY-TWO part 2:
If you have chosen Presentational and will
have a narrator, choose what type of
narration.

Keeping it simple, basically there are 3
types of narration- Omniscient, 1st person
and 3rd Person.

Omniscient narration.
With an Omniscient narrator, the Reader
is reading every character's thoughts (like
a god).

EXAMPLE: They all think this book is
helpful.

First person narration.
With first person narration, the Reader is
reading one character's thoughts from his
or her point of view.

EXAMPLE: -I hope this book is helpful.

Third person narration.
With third person narration, the Reader is
reading one character's thoughts but from
an outside point of view.

EXAMPLE: He/she/it believes this book is
helpful.

Please Note: with all types of narration,
the narrator needs to refer to the
characters by the same name each time
to avoid chaos for the reader.

EXAMPLE: If a character's name is William Stumped, the narrator must not call him William in one chapter and Bill in the next or Mr. Stumped on another page. With a Presentational narrator doing this, the Readers will become quickly confused.

Important note: Narrators Do NOT have to be truthful. But most Readers assume that they are.

STEP TWENTY-THREE:
Choose a level of character penetration for all your characters.
Again, keeping it simple, basically there are three levels of character penetration- Light, Deep and Cinematic.

Light character penetration.
The Reader reads one character's thoughts but does NOT feel or experience through his or her eyes.

EXAMPLE:" I'm relieved" This level of character penetration is good for minor characters.

Deep character penetration.
The Reader reads one character's thoughts and DOES feel and experience through his or her eyes.

EXAMPLE:" My legs become wobbly with the release of stress. I suddenly breathe so much better as if a huge weight is lifted from my chest. I feel elation well up and over me". This level of character penetration is excellent for major characters.

Cinematic View character penetration. The Reader reads from the viewpoint of all the characters, but never inside their mind's- similar to watching most movies.

STEP TWENTY-FOUR:
Choose an objective (a hook) for your story.
Decide what you're aiming for with this book or what is being sought after by telling this story? What's your goal for writing this book?

STEP TWENTY-FIVE:
Decide what will dominate in your story. Keeping it simple, basically there are four things that usually dominate a story- Plot, Characters, Style of writing or the Idea/Mood.
It's best to have all these elements in your story, but which do you want to really stick out? When you choose what you want to dominate, focus on this when writing, having more than half your chapters written with this in mind.

STEP TWENTY-SIX:
Choose a story theme. This is not to be confused with what is dominant or with factors being focused on within chapters. This is the overall theme of the entire book.

EXAMPLE: You can have a dominant

character story with many chapters focused on the factor of milieu with a theme of the idea of finding peace.

So back to choosing a story theme. Keeping it simple, basically there are five story themes-Plot, Effect, Style, Character and Idea.

Plot as a theme.
The overall theme of your story is on events and action. This is a very commercially successful choice. Think Indiana Jones.

Effect as a theme.
The overall theme of your writing is on the emotional mood and effect of the story.

Style as a theme.
The overall theme of your book is the style in which you write it.

Character as a theme.
The overall theme of your writing is on the main character. Again, the character's life becomes unbearable and the story's focus is on how he or she deals with that.

Idea as a theme.
The overall theme of your book is about an idea, in essence a book that makes the Reader think. If choosing Idea as a theme, please refer to step 27. If not, you can skip to step 28.

STEP TWENTY-SEVEN:
If you chose Idea as your story theme you will have to choose which type of idea theme.

Keeping it simple, basically there are 6 types of Idea themes -Moral Statement, Human Dignity, Social Comment, Human Nature, Human Relations and Innocence to Experience.

Moral statement idea story type.
A story that tries to persuade the reader to accept the idea of a moral principle.

Human Dignity idea story type.
A story focused on the struggle for human dignity. These books explore humanity's idea of dignity as a whole.

Social Comment idea story type.
A story that addresses problems with society and its ideas.

Human Nature idea story type.
A story that explores humanity and its ideas as a whole.

Please note: Character as a theme and Idea as a theme with the Idea type of human nature may seem similar but ARE different in that the Character as a theme is based on a one of a kind character compared to the Idea theme with the type of Human Nature is based on characters easily recognized in ourselves or anyone else.

Human Relations Idea story type.
A story based on how we get along with
one another and our individual ideas.

Innocence to Experience idea story type.
A story about growing up and how our
ideas change.

STEP TWENTY-EIGHT:
Decide in which category your story fits.
Keeping it simple, there are basically 2
types of categories for stories-
Contemporary literature and Traditional
plotted stories.

Contemporary literature.
A story where nothing is resolved. There's
a main question that is never answered.
This category uses a lot of symbolism to
tell a tale.

Traditional plotted story.
A story with no loose ends. A character
must do something after realizing
something he/she/it didn't know.
Decisions or actions are made to
dramatize what has changed from the
beginning.

STEP TWENTY-NINE:
Decide a structure for your book

Keeping it simple, basically there are 4
different kinds of writing structures-
Straight Chronological, Regular Recurring
Viewpoints, Multi point Chronological and

Parallel Running scenes.

Straight Chronological.
The Story starts at the beginning and shows major events in order. This structure has more clarity and consistency.

Regularly recurring viewpoints.
A set pattern of different point of views at each chapter IN THE SAME ORDER.

Multi viewpoint chronological.
The story is broken into clearly labeled parts. Each part is a period of time. Each chapter has a point of view different from the rest. Example: Spring, Summer, Fall, and Winter.

Parallel Running scenes.
TWO stories are going on at the same time alternating with each chapter and then coming together at the end.

STEP THIRTY PART ONE:
Decide what strategy to use for your chosen structure. Keeping it simple, basically there are 3 strategies for most book structures- Mosaic, Collage and Revelation.

Mosaic strategy for book structure.
Mosaic strategy is a pattern of images in your story. This strategy uses Symbols and repeated situations and/or attitudes.

Collage strategy for your book structure.

Collage uses a diverse collection of elements not related but connected somehow in the story.

Revelation strategy for your book structure.
Revelation has a main dynamic where a character realizes something that has been true all along. A secret is revealed/discovered.

Please Note: If choosing Revelation strategy for your book structure make sure of 4 things:

1.The secret revealed is worth knowing.

2.The secret must have a good build up.

3.Groundwork for the secret must be laid early in the story.

4. The secret must be hinted at throughout your story. Give the Reader a chance to guess but don't make it predictable.

If choosing Mosaic strategy for your book structure, please refer to step 30 PART 2.

STEP THIRTY PART TWO
Choose a format for your Mosaic Strategy for your book structure. There are basically 5 different formats for using the Mosaic strategy for book structure-Mood Piece, Character study, Slice of life, Theme and Allegory.

Mood Piece format for Mosaic strategy of book structure.
Mood piece formats sustain a mood throughout the story using a pattern of images, symbols, repeated situations or attitudes.

Character study format for Mosaic strategy of book structure.
Character study formats use each chapter of the story to develop a different character using their image, character related symbols or attitudes.

Slice of Life format for Mosaic strategy of book structure.
Slice of life tells the story about a certain way of life usually in a certain time period by using images, symbols situations and attitudes from its chosen time period. Example: The 1940s.

Theme format for your mosaic strategy of book structure.
Theme formats have a single concept in the story using images, symbols and repeated situations or attitudes to create a single theme.

Allegory formats for Mosaic strategy of book structure.
Allegories use a pattern of images, situations and attitudes of deeper meaning beyond the surface. This format has great symbolism, the characters have meanings beyond just themselves in the

story.

STEP THIRTY-ONE:
Decide if you want your story to be in a series. If so, decide what kind. Keeping it simple, basically there are 3 kinds of book series:

1. A book series with the same main character. You as a writer must invent new problems for the same character to solve.
EXAMPLE: Sherlock Holmes.

2. A book series that does not feature the same main character but has the same setting, family or universe. With this you as a writer need to leave something in the plot of each book unresolved to be taken up later by new different characters in the next book.

3. A series that has characters unsettled on personal issues so that they grow with each new book.

STEP THIRTY-TWO:
Choose a setting for your story. The setting is the surroundings in which your story takes place.

STEP THIRTY-THREE:
Create a game plan for both your Antagonist/hero and your Protagonist/villain.
Think about what they are both trying to do step by step.

STEP THIRTY-FOUR:
Make a list of 6-8 possible disasters and pick the least predictable of this list as your main plot. Try NOT to use the first thing that comes to your mind. Keep this list as reference for step 36.

STEP THIRTY-FIVE:
Choose a cause (create a background) for every effect (plot development) and/or disaster on the list created in step 34.

STEP THIRTY-SIX:
Choose at least 3 plot patterns for your story. You can have more of course, but it's usually better to have about three plots in a story-2 as sub plots and one as a main through line plot (Step 37). The Choices for Plots are numerous. Even attempting to keep it simple, there are about 25 different plots/sub plots patterns that should be mentioned.

1.Deliverance plot.
There's an unfortunate person, a threatener and a rescuer. A rescue for the condemned is accomplished. This is a staple plot choice for romances.

2.Revenge plot.
There's an avenger and a criminal. Revenge is carried out. This plot is one of the most emotionally powerful.

Please note: Revenge is mostly a personal retaliation as opposed to Vengeance (plot choice 3) which is usually serving justice for a wrong done to another.

3.Vengeance Plot.
Avenging the death or dishonor of a loved one, family member or friend by another loved one, family member or friend.

4.Pursuit plot.
There's a fugitive from justice threatened with capture and punishment.
Please note: Readers are more intrigued with characters that are falsely accused.

5.Disaster plot.
There's a vanquished power by a victorious enemy. A defeat is suffered such as a natural catastrophe or overthrown ruler. This is a popular plot choice for science fiction novels

6. Revolt plot.
There's a tyrant and a conspirator. There's a rebellion of some kind.

7. Daring enterprise plot:
There's a bold leader and a goal or sought object. This plot choice is in pretty much every adventure book you ever read.

8. Abduction plot.
There's an abductor, an abducted and a guardian. Kidnapping and rescuing of a captive. This is slightly different than a deliverance plot in the way that the abducted may save themselves.

9. The Enigma Plot.
There's an interrogator, a seeker and a problem. There's a search for a person or thing that must be found. A riddle must be solved. This is a primary plot choice for most mysteries and detective novels.

10. Obtaining plot.
There's a solicitor and an adversary who refuses to comply. Efforts to obtain are usually clever and dishonest means or unfair force.

11. Family Rivalry.
There's a preferred family member, a rejected family member and an object or person they both desire.

12. Murderous adultery plot.
There are usually two adulterers and the betrayed. The murder of a lover or spouse is committed.

13. Madness plot.
There's a mentally unstable person and a victim.

14. Fatal mistake plot.
There's an unwise or overly curious person, a victim and an object or person lost. There's misfortune to self or others as a result of carelessness, bad decision making or unreasonable curiosity.
Example: Pandora's box.

15. Involuntary crimes of love plot.
There's a lover, a beloved and a revealer.

There's unknowingly performed incest or adultery.

16. Self-sacrifice for an ideal plot.
There's a hero and an ideal. There's the sacrificing of one's self for the sake of honor, faith, duty or loyalty.

17. Self-sacrifice for kindred/family member or loved one plot.
There's a hero and a family member or loved one. Life or something of great value is sacrificed for a loved one/family member.

18. All sacrificed for passion plot.
There's a lover and the object of fatal passion. There's the ruin of fortunes or lives by a consuming passion or vice. Example: Drug addiction story.

19. Sacrifice of loved ones plot.
There's a hero, beloved victim and the necessity of the sacrifice.

20. Discovery of dishonor plot.
There's a guilty party and a discovery. There's the exposure of dark secrets and Love put to the test.

21. Obstacles to Love plot.
There are two lovers and on obstacle such as social status, keeping them apart.

22. An enemy loved plot.
There's the beloved enemy, the lover and a hater. Two lovers thwarted by family or

business hatred. Think Romeo and Juliet.

23. Ambition plot.
There's an ambitious person, a thing being coveted and adversary. This is different than daring enterprise plot in that there is a serious competitor not just difficult obstacles in the way.

24. Faulty judgment plot.
There's a mistaken one, the victim of the mistake and the cause of the mistake/guilty person. There's suspicion generated by an accident or by an enemy's design.

25.Recovery of lost loved one.
There's a seeker and the one found. There's the return of the one thought lost or dead. Loved ones are reunited.

STEP THIRTY-SEVEN:
Choose which of the three or more plot patterns previously chosen in step 36 will be the through line plot (the MAIN plot line of your story). Ask yourself what happens to the protagonist/hero to help you choose.

STEP THIRTY-EIGHT:
The remaining two or more plot choices will become your subplots.

Please Note: Plots are cause and effect. Plots are attitudes turning into motives, meeting resistance, creating conflict, with conflict leading to consequence. Deciding which causes and effects are more important to your story determines the difference between the main through line plot and the subplots.

STEP THIRTY-NINE:
Choose set pieces.
Set pieces are scenes in your story in which life, love, being true to one's self or an ideal, or the character's self-respect is at stake. In other words, DANGER scenes.

Set pieces must develop the character, increase emotion, explore your hook (the objective of the story) and connect the Reader to the main character.
These are usually the scenes you had in your head when first imagining your story. The pieces you can't wait to write.

STEP FORTY:
Create connections of people, objects or moods to bind one set piece to the next set piece. (Six degree your set pieces)

STEP FORTY-ONE:
With a pen, list all events that happen to your characters from the beginning of your story to the end. Keep this list for reference for steps 41,42 & etc.

STEP FORTY-TWO:
Go to your event list created with step 41. With a pencil, cross out all events that do not happen in the presence of the main character antagonist/hero.

STEP FORTY-THREE:
Try to combine the events remaining, as many as possible among the remaining events left on your event list edited in step 42.

STEP FORTY-FOUR:
Make connections of people, objects or moods to bind these combined events to the next event.

STEP FORTY-FIVE:
Choose which events from your edited list to turn into scenes that make it clear WHY your characters are doing what they do. Please Note: Choose action scenes FIRST and use scenes with dialog MORE than summary scenes.

STEP FORTY-SIX:
Make sure every scene must state a goal, introduce and develop conflict as well as have the main character having a disaster relevant to the book's climax.

STEP FORTY-SEVEN PART 1:
Write your scene goals on cards and fill out what the main character wants in each scene in 10 words or less.
State the conflict with who, where, for how long and at least 4 twists that the conflict could take. Also, on this card state the disaster. Use this for reference when writing each scene to help keep you on point.

STEP FORTY-SEVEN PART 2:
Try to link all scene goals together.

STEP FORTY-EIGHT:
In each scene's disaster, choose the scope of results, the immediacy of the results, the finality of the results and the result's direction.

STEP FORTY-NINE:
Put in as many fight scenes as possible while fitting with the vision of your story. Conflict is interesting.

STEP FIFTY:
With your scene goal cards as a reference, design segues to link every scene to the next. A segue is an uninterrupted transition from one scene to another (moving from one scene to another smoothly).

STEP FIFTY-ONE:
Think of ways to raise the stakes in each and every scene.

STEP FIFTY-TWO:
Cut out all scenes where characters are relaxed or calm.

STEP FIFTY-THREE:
Make sure all scenes are organized to be written with Goal, Conflict and Disaster IN THAT ORDER.

STEP FIFTY-FOUR:
Make sure all segues created in step 50

are organized to be written Emotion, Thought, Decision, Action IN THAT ORDER.

STEP FIFTY-FIVE:
Cut out all extra characters not needed for the scenes or segues chosen.

STEP FIFTY-SIX:
Set the scenes up so options for main characters dwindle.

STEP FIFTY-SEVEN:
Set scenes up so the main character is pulled farther away from the story goal with each scene.

STEP FIFTY-EIGHT:
Set up scenes that heap woes upon the main characters.

STEP FIFTY-NINE:
Set up scenes where assumptions are made by main characters that are not true.

STEP SIXTY:
Create plot complications and add terrible developments that are hidden from the Reader to be revealed later in the story.

STEP SIXTY-ONE:
Create clear back story, present story and hidden story plans for your book.

The back story is the history or background of the characters or environment of your story.

The present story is what is currently happening to the characters or environment of your story.

The hidden story is what is unknown to the Reader at first about the characters or environment of your story.

STEP SIXTY-TWO:
Have one or more scenes where the villain/protagonist seems to know more than the hero/antagonist.

STEP SIXTY-THREE:
Have a scene that shows the hero's thoughts about something were incorrect at least once. Having him/her/it make a mistake makes your hero more believable, relatable and causes the Reader to become anxious for your hero.

STEP SIXTY-FOUR:
Have a scene that puts a deadline on the major characters. Add pressure.

STEP SIXTY-FIVE:
Have a scene where a major character realizes that the stakes are higher than first thought. Add more consequence.

STEP SIXTY-SIX:
Have a scene where a major character realizes a whole new dimension to the previous disaster. Things are way worse than previously thought. Add more

despair.

STEP SIXTY-SEVEN:
Set up scenes as roadblocks so major
characters have to fight to get to the next
scene. Add more tension.

STEP SIXTY-EIGHT:
Have scenes that set up false alarms (You
can do this by having 3 similar scenes but
writing with the third having a different
result than the first two). This is done to
throw your Reader off and keep interest.

STEP SIXTY-NINE:
Have a scene where a major character
(and the Reader) expects something bad
but receives much worse.

STEP SEVENTY:
Have a scene where the villain/protagonist
introduces bad news calmly offhand. Add
shock.

STEP SEVENTY-ONE:
Decide if you want a prologue in your
story.
A prologue is an opening scene set in its
own chapter before the story's chapter
one.

Please note: You must have a strong
reason for a prologue. Prologues must
have the promise of conflict. Prologues
provide transition between two scenes
widely separated by time.

STEP SEVENTY-TWO:
Choose a dramatic scene for your
beginning that has the Major character in
a conflict in mid action.

Please Note: Always start your story as
late as possible before a disaster to snag
the Reader with the very first line of your
book.

STEP SEVENTY-THREE:
Write a beginning that promises the
Reader they'll be thrilled, uplifted,
entertained or scared.

STEP SEVENTY-FOUR:
Write a beginning that promises the
Reader they'll see the world from a
different point of view, they'll have
confirmed what they already believe about
this world or they'll learn about a more
interesting world.

STEP SEVENTY-FIVE:
Write a beginning that gives the Reader a
main character that will be in the main
action throughout the whole story.

STEP SEVENTY-SIX:
Design the opening scene to artfully
mirror the ending of your book.

STEP SEVENTY-SEVEN:
Choose your 2nd scene carefully. Keeping
it simple, basically there are three good
options for the 2nd scene.

2nd scene option 1.
Backfill.
Backfill is the background explaining who the characters are and how they came to the opening of the story.

2nd scene option 2:
Continuation of storyline.
The continuation of the storyline dramatizes whatever happens next to the main character.

2nd scene option 3.
Flashback.
Flashback should be used rarely to avoid confusing the Reader and must have a clear relation to the first scene.

STEP SEVENTY-EIGHT:
Decide how to present information in the middle of your story. Keeping it simple, basically there are 5 choices-Dialog, Description, Actions, Thoughts or Summary of actions. Pick one and stick to it as your main way of presenting information throughout your story.

STEP SEVENTY-NINE:
As you write, show EMOTION through description, example or discussion.

STEP EIGHTY:
As you write, show THOUGHT through review, analysis, planning or discussion THEN Action.

STEP EIGHTY-ONE:
Write a climax to your story.
The Climax is the big event that forces in
the story have been building towards.

Please note: The Climax MUST deliver
emotion and be logical to your plot. The
climax scene must grow naturally from
the actions that proceeded it. Climaxes
must be inevitable.

STEP EIGHTY-TWO:
Decide if you want a denouement.

Denouement is a section after the end of
your story that shows the consequences
of the plot and the fate of all characters.

Please note: denouements MUST be short
and have closure.

STEP EIGHTY-THREE:
REVISE your 1st draft using 6 different
tactics.

Revision tactic 1.
Wait at least 2 weeks and then read your
story as if you have never seen it. Then
analyze weaknesses. Fix them.

Revision tactic 2.
Remember steps 73 through 75? Trace
your Reader promises in the beginning,
the development of these promises in the
middle and the fulfillment of the promises
at the end.

Revision tactic 3.
Make sure EVERY scene advances the plot AND deepens the characters, if not fix them or remove them.

Revision tactic 4.
Use image patterns. Choose a prop (such as a street sign), an aspect of weather (like rain), or a symbol of culture. Make sure these images/items show up in a pattern early and are in the middle and end maybe even in your last line. This adds symbolism and depth to your story.

Revision tactic 5.
Rewrite. Replace plain ordinary words with their more intelligent counter parts.

EXAMPLE: Change "She is a little bit hopeful that this book will help other writers." to "She is partially optimistic that this novel can assist others like herself."

THEN cut out excess words. Say more with less.
"She's optimistic that this will assist others like her."

Revision tactic 6.
Polish your story. Double check your spelling, grammar and punctuation. Then have honest friends do the same. Be open to suggestion and correct any flaws.

STEP EIGHTY-FOUR:
Revise focusing on the word count. Keep novels between 60,000 and 90,000 words.

Publishers rarely print anything larger than that unless Stephen King or J.K. Rowling touched it.

STEP EIGHTY-FIVE PART ONE:
Revise linking ALL chapters to one another AND the end of the story.

STEP EIGHTY-FIVE PART TWO:
Revise focused on page count. Make sure each chapter is between 10 to 30 pages. Any longer usually tests the reader's attention span.

STEP EIGHTY-SIX:
Make sure the beginning and end has a good hook (maybe a quotable line).

STEP EIGHTY-SEVEN:
Revise so that ALL chapters end on a cliff hanger (suspenseful event) until the end.

STEP EIGHTY-EIGHT:
Revise so that the ending is memorable (possibly quote worthy) and artfully MIRRORS the beginning of your story.

Well, that's it. Hopefully you've accomplished the great 88 with ease. Optimistically, these steps created comprised from my creative writing notes can hopefully help you condense months or even years of education into a simple thought, organization and writing process you can follow over and over. I truly hope you'll utilize this ordinary guide and write many extraordinary books. Honestly please do, chances are high, I would love to read them.

-S. J. Russell

Author's Biography

My name is S.J. Russell. I'm an aspiring authoress that specializes in paranormal romance with a southern twist. I'm also a hobbyist artist, deist, lifestyle minimalist, island enthusiast, dependable momma and loyal wife not necessarily in that order. I live contently with my Wonderful husband and son in Georgia, USA.

If you enjoy my books and would like to contact me, please send caramel turtles -I mean letters to:

S.J. Russell
P.O. Box 23
Trion, GA. 30753

Or Email me at:
SJRussellauthor@aol.com

If you are interested in learning more about me, please visit my website at:
www.SJRussell.com

Or follow me on Facebook, Instagram, Twitter or Tumblr under the name S.J. Russell.

More of my books are available on Amazon.com and kindle stores worldwide.